MANDELSHTAM, Osip Emilévich. Osip Mandelstam; poems chosen and
tr. by James Greene. Shambhala (dist. by Random House), 1978
(c1977). 80p 78-58224. 4.95 pa ISBN 0-87773-136-5
Greene's translations bear the imprimatur of Mandelstam's widow,
Nadezhda, who praises them highly in a brief foreword. A second, longer
foreword by Donald Davies is very acute on the particular problems
involved in translating Mandelstam. Greene's own preface both instructs
the reader about where to turn for additional commentary in English and
makes his own translating criteria explicit: his aim is to produce texts that
will not only preserve the sense of the original but will work as poems in
English. In pursuit of this second goal, Greene resorts to the omission of
lines and whole stanzas rather than rendering them in poetically inadequate
translations. While this approach will somewhat limit the usefulness of
Greene's work for those seeking an aid to understanding the Russian
originals, the resulting translations have a remarkable aesthetic power. The
poems, a representative selection from all periods of Mandelstam's career,
are followed by a series of explanatory notes that are instructive in
themselves and that further help to situate Greene's work in the body of
Mandelstam criticism in English. For those who must read Mandelstam in
translation and who want to know what all the excitement is about,
Greene's translations are highly recommended.

Osip Mandelstam

Osip Mandelstam

Poems Chosen and Translated by
JAMES GREENE

Forewords by
Nadezhda Mandelstam & Donald Davie

SHAMBHALA
Boulder · 1978

Shambhala Publications, Inc.
1123 Spruce Street
Boulder, Colorado 80302

© 1977 James Greene. All rights reserved.
ISBN 0-87773-136-5
LCC 78-58224

Distributed in the United States by Random House
and in Canada by Random House of Canada Ltd.

Printed in the United States of America

*The cover photograph of derelict barges in Petrograd, 1922,
is reproduced courtesy of Radio Times, Hulton Picture Library, London.*

For C., R., and V.; and for P.

Contents

from STONE (1913)

from TRISTIA (1922)

from POEMS (1928)

Poems published posthumously

Foreword by
Nadezhda Mandelstam

The most difficult task in the world is the translation of verses, particularly of a true poet — in whose verses there is no discrepancy between the form and the content, both of them always new. This is particularly the case with Mandelstam who, unlike *innovators* such as Mayakovsky and Pasternak (who, because they were innovators, were easily aped), composed verses *in tradition*, which is far more difficult to imitate. Mr Robert Lowell's translations of Mandelstam are very free; Mr Paul Celan's into German also free. Both are a very far cry from the original text. As far as I know the translations of Mr Greene are some of the best I ever saw. (I can't give my opinion about the Italian translations, as I don't know Italian as well as English, French and German.)

Mandelstam said that the contents are squeezed from the form as water from a sponge. If the sponge is dry, there would be no moisture at all. So, to render the content — which Mr Greene has succeeded in doing — is to give, in a way, the form or harmony, the harmony which *can't* be rendered in translation, the harmony which is simple and at the same time mysteriously complicated.

NOTE: Nadezhda Mandelstam wrote this after seeing an early version of the manuscript. The versions printed here are probably more harmonious and 'free' (and therefore more 'faithful') than the ones she was commenting on. But as she is not the easiest person in the world to communicate with (letters sent through the post to Moscow do not reach her), I do not know what she would make of my final transcriptions.
— J.G.

Foreword by Donald Davie

Of Mandelstam's *Octets*, Robert Chandler has said that 'the informing energy of the poem stems from, is a part of, the universal impulse to form, which leads equally to the creation of a petal or a cupola, the pattern of a group of sailing-boats or a poem.' And Mr Chandler may be right. Yet as I worked at the *Octets** it seemed to me on the contrary that Mandelstam was distinguishing one kind of form from another, and was celebrating only those forms that are 'bent in', arced, the form of a foetus or a cradle, specifically *not* the open-ended and discontinuous mere 'pattern' (rather than 'form') that a group of sailing-boats may fall into.

I stress this because I am inclined to see in it the clue to what is distinctive about this poet, and what is distinctively daunting about the challenge he presents to his translators. If I am right, Mandelstam's poems themselves yearn towards, and achieve, forms that are 'bent in', rounded, sounding a full bell-note. Moreover, because what the poems say is at one with the forms they find for the saying, we see why it is that, as Clarence Brown tells us, for Mandelstam 'cognition' is always 'recognition' — re-cognition, a return upon itself, a 'coming round again'.

And nothing else, so far as I can see, will enable us to reconcile Anna Akhmatova's firm declaration, 'he had no poetic forerunners', with his widow's no less firm admonition: 'Mandelstam . . . unlike *innovators* such as Mayakovsky and Pasternak . . . composed verses *in tradition*, which is far more difficult to imitate'. What sort of a poet can this be, who is 'traditional' and yet has 'no poetic forerunners?' We solve this riddle by saying that in his techniques Mandelstam was indeed unprecedented, yet the techniques were made to serve a *form* — why not say simply, a *beauty?* — that rejoiced in calling upon every precedent one might think of, from Homer to Ovid, to the builders of Santa Sophia, to Dante and Ariosto and Racine. For it is true, surely: the sort of form to which Mandelstam vows himself alike in nature and in

---

* Donald Davie's version of Mandelstam's long poem *The Octets* has been published in *Agenda*, Vol. 14, No. 2, 1976.

art, the form of the bent-in and the rounded-upon-itself, is the most ancient and constant of all European understandings of the beautiful — it is what long ago recognized in the circle the image of perfection. This profoundly traditional strain and aspiration in Mandelstam explains why the Russia of his lifetime is seldom imaged directly in his poetry, and why, when it is so imaged, the image is overshadowed by others from ancient Greece or from Italy; it explains why domes and cupolas and shells (whether whorled or scalloped) appear in his poetry so often; and it explains why the hackneyed figures of the sky as a dome and a vault, and of the sea as curved round the earth's curve, appear in that poetry so insistently and with such otherwise unexplained potency. If we were to call Mandelstam 'classical' this is what we might mean, or what we ought to mean. And nothing is further from what may reasonably be seen as the characteristic endeavour of the Western European and American of this century, in all the arts — that is to say, the finding of beauty in the discontinuous and the asymmetrical, the open-ended and indeed the adventitious.

Just here arises the peculiarly extreme difficulty of translating Mandelstam into English. Before James Greene's, the most readable and accomplished translation we had was by W. S. Merwin, done in collaboration with Clarence Brown. But this was, necessarily and properly, an *American* translation; a translation, that's to say, into that one of the twentieth-century idioms which is, and has been ever since Walt Whitman, and even in such an untypical American as Pound, pre-eminently vowed to the open-ended and the discontinuous. Yet Mandelstam is the most 'European' of all Russian poets since Pushkin. How could Merwin have succeeded? Yet he did — to the extent that he does indeed bring over, for a public that has not and cannot have any immediate access to the Mediterranean fountains of European consciousness, as much of Mandelstam as can survive that oceanic passage. Here however was a chance for that one of the English-speaking idioms which *is* part of the European consciousness: could the British idiom achieve what by its very nature the American could not? James Greene had his own difficulties; for current British idioms, insofar as they respect the integrity of the verse-line and the verse-stanza (and plainly that was what was involved), characteristically give *pattern* instead of *form*, or else

— to put it another way — they preserve the arc of the poem's form only by 'filling in', by not having the content of the poem pressing up against the curve of its form with equal pressure at every point. (The opposite danger, which I have not escaped in my versions, is of packing the content against the verse-line so tightly that the verse is felt to be straining and as it were bursting at the seams.) James Greene was equal to the challenge. His measuring up to it is shown in the first place by his daring to do what every verse-translator must have guiltily felt he ought to do, but was afraid of doing — that's to say, by leaving untranslated those parts of poems for which he could find no equivalent in English verse that carried authority. His more positive virtues — particularly in finding English near-equivalents for the punning resemblances in sound which, for Mandelstam as for Pasternak, function as structural principles, given the richly orchestrated nature of Russian . . . these can be appreciated only by those who can check back against the Russian originals.

Here for the first time we have a faithful version, not of Mandelstam, but of as much of Mandelstam as this scrupulous translator is prepared to stand by — faithful as never before, because as never before there is no line of the Russian poems that is not made *poetry* in English. Previous British versions have been wooden; this one *rings* — it is bronze, properly Roman bronze.

Stanford University, California

Translator's Preface

I

'[Mandelstam] had no poetic forerunners – wouldn't that be something worth thinking about for his biography? In all of world poetry, I know of no other such case. We know the sources of Pushkin and Blok, but who will tell us where that new, divine harmony, Mandelstam's poetry, came from?'

Anna Akhmatova

'Mandelstam is perhaps the fifth of the five (or six or seven) Russian poets whose verse can furnish virtually palpable pleasure to anyone who enjoys poetry.'

Andrew Field, *The Complection of Russian Literature*, 1971

Anyone who wants to know Mandelstam must read his poems; for knowledge *about* him, and his times, Clarence Brown's *Mandelstam* (1973) and the two volumes of Nadezhda Mandelstam's memoirs, *Hope Against Hope* and *Hope Abandoned* (1971 and 1974), are invaluable. Briefly, he was born in 1891 in Warsaw of (non-religious) Jewish parents and spent his childhood and adolescence in St Petersburg; he studied in Paris and Heidelberg and travelled to Italy (1907–10), and subsequently was marooned within the Soviet Union.

Mandelstam was associated with the poetic grouping known as 'Acmeism' (whose 'members' also included Gumilyov and Akhmatova), marshalled against the other-worldliness of Symbolism as represented pre-eminently by Alexander Blok. Acmeism was a kind of Imagism, aiming too at poems that would be precise, concrete, and 'architectural'. But just as the tenets of Imagism are not easily discernible in, say, the Pound of the Cantos, there is nothing programmatic in Mandelstam's actual poems either: they perpetually weigh anchor and sail towards *terra incognita*, 'the charm of something never yet said'; if a poem can be paraphrased, Mandelstam said, the sheets have not been rumpled, there poetry has not spent the night. Writing (perhaps also *reading*) a poem, he said in an essay on Dante, is like running across the whole width of a river jammed with Chinese junks sailing in various directions: 'the sense of a poem leaps from junk to junk in making its way across the river' (Clarence Brown).

Mandelstam's poems — like some of Valéry's — resonate with silence, like pebbles under water; his diction, like Pope's, pure as sand. They span thirty years and record the echo in his luminous mind of St Petersburg and Western Europe before the First World War, of the Russian Revolution and Civil War, of Stalinism and the 'non-vegetarian' purges of the thirties. When challenged, in 1937, to define Acmeism, Mandelstam called it 'a home-sickness for world culture'.

He was last seen in December 1938, feeding off the garbage heap of a transit camp near Vladivostok; and the survival of many of his poems (some hidden in saucepans and old shoes, some preserved because his wife, Nadezhda, had learnt them by heart) is something of a miracle.

Like an alchemist, he transmuted into gold his own experiences of arrest, interrogation, exile (from Moscow to Voronezh) and persecution: as he said in his poem of 1912 about the cathedral of Notre Dame in Paris (No. 39):

> I too one day will create
> Beauty from cruel weight.

In some verses written as a joke in 1935 he indicated what his official fate would be in the Soviet Union:

> What street is this?
> — 'This is Mandelstam Street.
> His morals weren't exactly "sweet-as-a-flower".
> That's why this street — or rather sewer
> Or, rather, slum —
> Has been named after
> Osip Mandelstam.'

After Stalin's death, Mandelstam was 'rehabilitated'; a Soviet edition of his poems (with omissions, including the ones noted below) came out in 1974; but there is still, of course, no street anywhere in the Soviet Union named after Osip Mandelstam.

II

'Translation it is that openeth the window, to let in the light; that breaketh the shell, that we may eat the kernel.'

Preface to the King James Bible, 1611

The question of how to translate — should translations, like husbands, be 'faithful' or 'free'? — has continued to be controversial ever since the literal-minded Gavin Douglas rebuked Caxton for his 'counterfeit' of Virgil, and Dryden (two hundred years later) aligned himself cautiously on the other side: '. . . something must be lost in all Transfusion, that is, in all Translation.' Where I have added 'From' to the number in brackets at the bottom of each poem, this is to indicate that, in these versions, lines (and sometimes whole stanzas) will have been suppressed, in the interests of producing a poem that works *in English:* as Pound's transformations of Rihaku do, however dubious his 'scholarship'. In one instance I have compressed two of Mandelstam's poems — Nos 131 and 132 — into one. I have usually tried to keep as close as possible to Mandelstam's flesh and bones and blood, but — allying myself with Dryden rather than Douglas (and, more optimistically than either, hoping that something may even occasionally be gained by transplantation) — always bearing in mind what Dante Gabriel Rossetti said: 'the life-blood of . . . translation is this, — that a good poem shall not be turned into a bad one.' Henry Gifford, in his introduction to Charles Tomlinson's *Versions from Fyodor Tyutchev* (1960), writes about 'liberties of the translator, but liberties assumed for the sake of a new order . . . For a new poem the version must be: otherwise it cannot live. Translation is resurrection, but not of the body.'

Mandelstam's poems are rhymed and strictly metrical, *The man who found a horseshoe* being the only exception I can think of. I have mostly had to eschew rhyme (but not half-rhyme, internal rhymes or assonance), and have tried to feel my way towards what might be the right rhythm for English. Some may say that my 'from' versions are not translations at all but 'adaptations' or 'imitations'. (Personally I find debatable the boundaries between these soi-disant distinct terms — at least, difficult to establish rigidly: is the Authorised Version of the Bible a translation

* But see Donald Davie's version of *The Octets* (composed 1933–35) — which can usefully be compared with John Riley's (Grosseteste, 1976) to my ear unrhythmical, 'American', version.

or adaptation?). Poems Nos 33 and 34, for example, are both sonnets in the original; in my renditions they contain ten and three lines respectively. However, in planting Mandelstam's trees over again in foreign soil, I hope I have not deviated too much from his sense or spirit.

To the non-Russian-speaking reader who wants to know about the relation between Mandelstam's metres (which I have not consciously set out to re-enact), length of line, etc., and mine, I can only say: 'decisions' of this kind are made intuitively, or in heaven; don't eat my — or any other translator's — menus or pontifical recipes; *total* 'faithfulness', were it possible — the 'same' metre, rhyme-scheme, pattern of sounds, number of syllables, line-length, etc., etc. — would be an absurdity. As D. M. Thomas says in the Introduction to his translations of Anna Akhmatova's *Requiem* and *Poem Without a Hero* (Elek, 1976), 'it is simplistic to imagine that form can be translated from one language to another, lock, stock and barrel, as though by removal van.'

In October 1816 Keats was first looking into Chapman's Homer. A line describing the shipwrecked Ulysses ('The sea had soak'd his heart through'), which evinced from him a shout of delight, is actually an interpolation of Chapman's. As far as I know, I have gone in more for subtraction than addition, but, in any case, there may be several morals in this story.

The Russian text I have used, and the numbering of Mandelstam's poems given in brackets at the bottom of each poem, come from his *Sobraniye Sochineniy (Collected Works)*, Vol. 1 (2nd ed., revised and expanded, 1967), ed. Gleb Struve and Boris Filippov, Inter-Language Literary Associates, Washington. Titles of poems correspond to Mandelstam's, except those given in brackets, which I have added. Thirty-one of the poems printed here are not among those translated by Clarence Brown and W. S. Merwin in *Osip Mandelstam; Selected Poems*, Oxford University Press, 1973. Of those that are, anyone who wants to compare my versions with theirs has only to look at the numbers printed at the *top* of the poems in their volume.

The Soviet edition of 1974 is not as comprehensive as the American. Of the poems translated here the Soviet edition excludes Nos 165, 194, 307, 341, 347, 351, 352, 353, 357, 362, 368, 372, 380, 383, 385 and 387, some for what must be ideological reasons.

I have included none of Mandelstam's 1932 poems, which some consider to be his finest: this is because I don't and because I am not attracted to the scientific imagery of some of his poems of the early 1930s (nor do I think it translatable)*, nor to what Donald Rayfield (who *is* in sympathy with them) has called his 'Kultur and Travelogue' poems.

J.G.

Acknowledgements

I am indebted to Antony Wood of Paul Elek Ltd, for his interest in this project, his editorial patience and perseverance.

I would like to thank William Cookson, Martin Dodsworth, Ian Hamilton and Tom Wharton for permission to reprint those of my translations which first appeared, sometimes in earlier versions, in *Agenda*, *English*, *The New Review*, and *Poetry and Audience*.

I am indebted to Mina Balaskas, Robert and Sonya Chandler, Alison Herford, Natalie Rinne and Maxwell Shorter for illuminating some of the obscurities in the Russian of some of these poems. Robert Chandler with his superior knowledge of Russian magnanimously came to my rescue many times, and in my Notes I have drawn on his insights contained in an unpublished article on Mandelstam and Ezra Pound.

In 1976 a Philadelphia Association study-group on Mandelstam, which I was responsible for, helped me to see some of my own errors in slow-motion.

I want to thank G.A., A.B., C.B., D.B., I.B., J.B., K.B., C.D., M.D., M.H., M.H., L.L., R.L., K.M., J.P., N.R., T.R., C.T., D.W. and T.W. for their hospitality at various times to versions of these versions.

Many friends who don't know Russian have examined the MS, or parts of it, in various phases of its vision or revision, with Leavis-like scrutiny: my debt to Fyodor Cherniavsky, Michael Cohen, Jan Farquharson and Gerald Guinness is immeasurable.

Professors Donald Davie and Henry Gifford, whom I do not know and who know Russian, were kind enough to read the MS carefully and encouragingly and to point out some of my mistakes; as did Stephen Fender, Peter Levi and Donald Rayfield, all of whose detailed and telling comments enabled me to transform the text considerably. I have made wide use, too, in my Notes, of Donald Rayfield's valuable writings on Mandelstam.

I do not know what I would have done without Graham Martin, or Eric Harber (who mercilessly picked holes), or Colin Falck, and their judicious, stringent and always generous perspectives. If these translations work, it will be in large measure due to them; if they don't, I am unredeemable.   — J.G.

from

STONE

(1913)

Fruit breaking loose from tree —
Hollow, muffled, gingerly — ,
The silent sound
Of forest all around . . .

[1]   1908

Suddenly, from the half-dark hall,
You slipped out in a light shawl —
The servants slept on,
We disturbed no one . . .

[3]   1908

To cherish only children's books,
Childish dreams & cogitations; throw
Out anything grown-up & clocks:
Grow out of deeply-rooted sorrow.

I am tired to death
Of life, & welcome nothing it can give me.
But I adore the poor earth:
There is no other earth to see.

In a garden far-off I swung
On a simple wooden swing,
And I remember dark tall firs
In hazy fevers.

[4]　1908

April-blue enamel:
Inconspicuous
And pale,
A birch-tree hammocks in the evening sky.

Fine netting cuts
Thin patterns perfectly:
Designs on porcelain plates
Traced keenly

By courteous
Artist on a firmament of glass,
Knowing his short-lived strength —
Unconscious of sad death . . .

[6]   1909

4

What shall I do with the body I've been given,
So much at one with me, so much my own?

For the calm happiness of breathing, being able
To be alive, tell me where I should be grateful?

I am gardener, flower too, and un-alone
In this vast dungeon.

My breath, my glow, you can already see
On the windowpanes of eternity.

A pattern is imprinted there,
Unknown till now.

Let this muddle die down, this sediment flow out.
The lovely pattern cannot be crossed out.

[8]   1909

An inexpressible sadness
Opened two huge eyes;
The vase, woken-up,
Splashed crystal:

Flowers filled all the room
With languor — spicy syrup!
Such a little kingdom
To swallow so much sleep.

Red wine in the sunlight,
May weather —
While white fine fingers
Break the thin biscuit . . .

[9]   1909

New-mown ears of early wheat
In level rows;
Fingers thrill & press against
Fingers fragile as themselves.

[*Unpublished in the Struve/Filippov editions*]   1909

Silence
Of the brute-dark soul:
Sad and good

Silence
Like young dolphins
Sounding the grey gulfs, the world

[*from* 11]   1909

SILENTIUM

It has not yet come into being —
The music and the word
To genuinely join
Whatever is in the world
From the beginning.

The breasts of the sea
Heave harmoniously;
The clear day sparkles like a lunatic;
Spray of lilac,
Pale in bowl of clouded blue.

In aboriginal silence
May my lips bring forth
A shining sound which, pure of birth,
May score my words. —
Persist as salt, o spray of worlds,
You, Aphrodite, the crystal, the *immaculata!*

[*from* 14]   1910

Ears stretch a sensitive sail,
Dilated eyes empty,
And unresounding birds
Sail the midnight sea.

Like nature I am poor,
Scatterbrained like the sky,
And my freedom shadowy
Like the voice of a midnight bird.

I see the unbreathing moon
And a sky deader than canvas;
Your strange and morbid world
I welcome, emptiness!

[15]   1910

Sultry dusk covers the couch,
Lungs inhale distress . . .
Dearest of all to me, perhaps,
Are delicate cross, secret path

[19]   1910

Horses stepping slow
Through this dark-candled night,
These strange ones surely know
Where they are taking me.

Confident of their concern,
At the bend I am thrown,
Suddenly,
Towards star-light . . .

[*from* 20]   1911

[LAPSE]

Light sows a meagre beam
Coldly in the sodden forest.
I carry slowly in my heart
The grey bird, sadness.

What shall I do with the wounded bird?
The earth is effaced, silent, dead.
From the belfry masked by mist
Somebody stole the bells.

Dumb & bereaved
The high air stands,
A white & empty mound
Of quietness & mist.

The morning's tenderness — half reverie, half real —
Is never-ending.
Miracle of drowsiness & lull:
Mist-like thoughts are ringing . . .

[21]   1911

11

THE SEA-SHELL

It may be — night —
You have no need of me; out of the world's abyss,
Like a shell without pearls,
I am hurled on your shores.

In equanimity you stir the waves
And obstinately chant;
But you will loyally esteem
This lying, unnecessary, thing,

And lie down on the sand nearby,
Wrap your chasuble around,
And bind to the sea-shell
The colossal bell of the billows.

And the walls of the delicate shell,
Like the house of a tenantless heart,
Your whispering spray will splash
And wind and rain and mist . . .

[26]   1911

In the haze your image
Trembled,
Troubled
And eluded me:
'Good God!' I said, unthinkingly.
The name of the Lord — a large bird —
Surged
Through my breast.

In front: a swirl of mist.
Behind: the empty cage.

[30]   1912

No, not the moon, but the bright clock-face
Shines on me. Am I guilty
If the delicate stars strike me as *milky?*

And the loftiness of Batyushkov strikes me as base:
When asked the time, his answer was —
'Eternity'.

[31]   1912

THE ONE WHO WALKS

Dark perpendiculars fill me
With uncontrollable terror.
I am delighted with the swallow in the sky,
And I like the way the bell-towers soar!

And it seems to me, the age-old plodding one,
On winding paths, above the precipice,
I hear the snowball grow,
Timelessness strike on clocks of stone.

If it could be! But I am not that wayfarer
Flashing past on fading foliage,
Genuine sadness sings in me;

An avalanche is in the hills!
And all my self is in the bells.
But music cannot save from the abyss!

[32]   1912

14

THE CASINO
[unpremeditated happiness]

The wind is playing with a corrugated cloud,
The anchor scrapes the ocean bottom; lifeless
As linen, my wine-struck mind
Hangs over an abyss.

But I revel in the casino on the dunes:
The vast view from the misty window,
A thin ray of light on the crumpled tablecloth.

And, with greenish water suspended all around,
When the wine flashes crystal like a rose,
I like to soar — the grey gull's shadow!

[*from* 33]   1912

[AWE]

Few live for Always.
But if the passing moment makes you anxious
Your lot is terror & your house precarious!

[*from* 34]   1912

THE LUTHERAN

I met a funeral, on a walk,
Last Sunday by the Lutheran church.
An absent-minded passer-by, I stood to watch
Rigorous distress on the faces of the flock.

I could not understand their words,
And nothing shone except gaunt bridles
And the dimness of the horses' hooves
Reflecting off the toneless Sunday side-roads.

In the tenacious half-light of the carriage
Where sadness, the dissembler, lay entombed,
Wordless and tearless and grudging even greeting
A buttonhole of autumn roses gleamed.

Black-ribboned foreigners kept step,
And ladies weak from weeping went on foot,
Red faces veiled. Above,
The coachman drove straight on.

Whoever you are, Lutheran now deceased,
Your funeral rites were rendered artlessly:
A decorous tear misted all eyes duly;
With constraint the bells rang out.

I thought — no need to be rhetorical:
We are not prophets, nor precursors,
Neither delight in heaven nor live in fear of hell;
And in dull noon we burn like candles.

[37]   1912

AYA-SOPHIA

Aya-Sophia — here the Lord ordained
That emperors & nations should halt!
In fact your dome, a witness said,
Hangs from heaven by a chain.

All ages take their measure from Justinian:
Diana, from her shrine in Ephesus, allowed
One hundred & seven green marble pillars
To be pillaged for a foreign god.

How did your bountiful builder feel
When — with open hands & loftly spirit —
He set the apses & the chapels,
Pointing them to West & East?

A splendid temple, bathing in the world —
A festival of light from forty windows;
Under the dome, on pendentives, the four Archangels
Sailing onward, lovelier than the world.

And this sage & spherical building
Will outlive nations & their centuries.
Nor will the seraphs' resonant sobbing
Warp the dark gilt surfaces.

[38]   1912

NOTRE DAME

Where a Roman judged a foreign people
A basilica stands and, first and joyful
Like Adam once, an arch plays with its own ribs:
Groined, muscular, never-unnerved.

From outside, the bones betray the plan:
Flying buttresses decide
That cumbersome mass shall never crush the wall:
Onslaught of a crashing vault is hindered.

Elemental labyrinth, unfathomable forest,
The Gothic soul's rational abyss,
Egyptian power with Christian shyness,
Where perpendicular is potentate.

But the more attentively I studied,
Notre Dame, your monstrous ribs, your stronghold,
The more I thought: I too one day will create
Beauty from cruel weight.

[*from* 39]   1912

Bitter bread, and blazing arid air.
Wounds impossible to bind!
Joseph, sold into Egypt, could not have pined
With more despair!

Bedouin under the starry sky,
Eyes shut, on horses,
Improvise
Out of the troubles of the day gone by.

Images lie close at hand:
He traded horses;
I lost my quiver in the sand.
Haze of happenings disperses.

If genuinely sung,
Whole-heartedly — at last
Nothing is left
But space, and stars, and song!

[54]   (1913)

Nature is Roman, & mirrors Rome.
We see its images of civic grandeur
As in an azure circus in the pigeon-filled air,
Colonnades of groves, fields to form a forum.

Nature is Roman, & it seems
Vainglorious now to trouble any god:
There are entrails of sacrifice to guess at wars,
Slaves to be silent, stones to build!

[65]　1914

Sleeplessness . . . Homer, stretched sails.
I have counted half the catalogue of ships —
The expansive shoal, the flight of birds, the canvas
Shrouding Hellas.

Like a concourse of cranes toward far-off borders
(On the heads of kings the spray of gods)
Where are you sailing? To you — but for Helen —
What could Troy mean, Achaean men?

All is moved by love: Homer, the sea.
To which shall I listen? Homer speaks silently.
And the black sea, like an orator,
Pounds up my pillow with a roar.

[78]　1915

Herds of horses gaily neigh or graze,
The valley rusts like Rome:
Transparent rapids bear away the years,
The un-wet gold of classical Spring days.

This Autumn, trampling oak-leaves
Thick on deserted paths,
I remember Caesar's lovely profile:
Effeminate features, treacherous hook-nose.

Forum and Capitol are far away,
Nature is quietly drooping:
Even here, on the world's rim, I hear
The years of Augustus turn like orb or apple.

When I am old may my sadness gleam.
I was born in Rome; it has come back to me;
My she-wolf was kind Autumn;
August — month of the Caesars — smiled on me.

[80]   1915

You are trapped — hunters lured you:
Stag, forests weep for you!

Sun, confiscate my black coat:
But my staying-power keep safe, keep safe my heart!

(*from* 165)   1913

[MORTIFICATION]

The ancients of Euripides, an abject throng,
(I go the *snake's* way)
Shuffle off like sheep.
In my heart — dark injury.

But it will not be long
Before I shake off sadness
Like a boy in the evening
Shaking sand from his sandals.

(*from* 178)   1914

from

TRISTIA
(1922)

— How the splendour of these veils and of this dress
Weighs me down in my disgrace!

     — In stony Troezen there will be
     A celebrated coming-to-grief,
     The steps of the imperial stairs
     Will blush,

     . . . .

    . . . .

     And a black sun rise
     For the amorous mother.

— O if it were hatred seething in my breast —
But you see — the confession flew from my own lips.

     — In broad daylight
     Phaedra burns with a black flame.
     In broad daylight
     Smoke of a funeral torch.
     Beware of your mother, Hippolytus:
     Phaedra — the night — watches you
     In broad daylight.

— With my black love I have sullied the sun . . .
. . . .

     — We are afraid and do not dare
     Succour the imperial grief.
     Stung by Theseus
     Night assaulted him.
     We shall take the dead home
     With our burial song,
     And cool the black sun
     Of a savage — insomniac — passion.

[82]   1916

24

Basilicas where virgins
Contrapuntally are chanting!
Stone vaults to usher in
A vision of eyebrows: arch-shaped, lofty & enchanting!

On the ramparts aggrandized with archangels
I survey the city from a marvellous eminence;
Within the walls of the acropolis crossed with sadness
For Russian loveliness & Russian names.

Isn't it wonderful that we dream of a garden
Where pigeons are soaring through a hot blue sky,
A nun tenderly singing the Orthodox chants:
The ardent Cathedral of the Assumption, here Moscow
        is Florence.

These polyphonic churches with Italianate soul
(Snowed-under, five-domed: their Russian grace-notes!)
Are Aurora's arrival —
In a fur-coat!

[*from* 84]   1916

We shall leave our bones in transparent Petropolis,
Where Proserpina rules over us.
We drink the deadly air with every breath,
And every hour is the anniversary of our death.
Goddess of the sea, thunderous Athena,
Remove your mighty helmet of stone.
In transparent Petropolis we shall leave our bones:
Here Proserpina is czar.

[89]   1916

26

With no confidence in miracles of resurrection,
We wandered through the cemetery.
— Here the earth, you know, ubiquitously
Reminds me of those hills

.   .   .   .

.   .   .   .

Where Russia stops abruptly
Above the black and god-forsaken sea.

An ample field escapes
Down these monastic slopes;
I did not want to leave the spacious Vladimir
To travel south,
But to stay with that lacklustre nun,
In the dark (the wooden)
Village of god's fools,
Would have been to court disaster.

I kiss your sunburnt elbow
And a wax-like patch of forehead —
Still white, I know,
Under a strand of dark-complexioned gold.
I kiss your hand whose bracelet
Leaves a strip of white:
Tauris's ardent summers
Work such wonders.

How quickly you became a dark one
And came to the Redeemer's meagre icon
And couldn't be torn away from kissing —
You who in Moscow had been the proud one.
Music remains,
A miraculous sound.
Here, take this sand:
I am pouring it from hand to hand.

[90]   1916

27

Out of the bottle the stream of golden honey poured
So leisurely that she had time to murmur
(She who had invited us): Here, in sad Tauris where fate has
　　led us,
We will not be bored. — She glanced over her shoulder.

Everywhere the rites of Bacchus, as if the world is only
　　watchmen, dogs;
You'll not meet anyone;
Like heavy barrels the peaceful days roll on:
Far-off voices in a hut — you neither understand them
　　nor reply.

After tea we came into the great brown garden,
Dark blinds lowered like eyelids on the windows,
Past white columns to see the grapes
Where sun-lit glass has sluiced the sleepy mountain.

The vine, I said, lives on like ancient battles —
Leafy-headed horsemen fight in flowery flourishes.
Knowledge of Hellas is here in stony Tauris —
And the golden acres, the rusty furrows.

Well, in the white room silence stands like a spinning-wheel.
It smells of paint and vinegar and cellar-cooled wine.
Do you recall, in the Grecian house, the wife dear to all —
Not Helen, the other? It was *time* she embroidered.

Golden fleece, where are you, golden fleece?
The whole journey a thundering of the sea's weighty waves.
And leaving his ship, canvas worn-out on the seas,
Odysseus came back, filled with time and space.

[92]　　1917

Spring's clear-grey
Asphodels
Are still far away.
Meanwhile sand rustles, waves seethe.
But, like Persephone, my whole soul will join
The light-hearted circle:
In the kingdom of the dead you cannot unearth
Delightful arms sun-burnt as these.

Why do we entrust to a boat
The funeral urn's full weight,
And celebrate the black rose festivals
On amethyst-coloured waters?
My whole soul aspires there,
Unto the promontory in the mist,
And a black sail will come back from there
After the burial!

Quickly storm clouds pass
In an unlit column,
Under a windy moon
Black rose-flakes are flying.
Over the ship's cypress side
Memory's huge flag —
Bird of death and mourners —
Trails its black borders.

And the sad fan of years gone by
Opens with a rustling sigh
Where the amulet was darkly buried
With a shudder in the sand.
My whole soul aspires there,
Unto the promontory in the mist,
And a black sail will come back from there
After the burial!

[93]   1917

TRISTIA

I have taken to heart the lesson of goodbyes
In bareheaded laments in the night.
Oxen chew, waiting lengthens,
The last hour of the watch in the city.
And I bow to ceremonial cock-crowing nights
When lifting their lading of grief for the journey
Eyes red with crying search the horizon
And singing of Muses blends with the weeping
        of women.

Who can know from the word 'goodbye'
What kind of separation lies before us,
Or what the cock's clamour promises
When a light burns in the acropolis
And in his stall the lazy ox chews:
Why the cock,
The herald of new life,
Beats on the city walls with his wings?

And I like the way of weaving:
The shuttle comes and goes, the spindle hums,
And — flying to meet us like swan's down —
Look, barefooted Delia comes!
Oh how meagre the basis of life,
How threadbare the language of elysium!
Everything existed of old, everything
        recurs anew,
The flash of recognition is all that we welcome.

So be it: a translucent manikin
On a clean clay plate —
A squirrel's stretched-out skin:
Bent over the wax, a girl examines it.
Not for us to guess at Grecian Erebus:

For women wax, what bronze is for men.
On us our fate falls only in battles;
Their death they die in divination.

[104]   1918

Wasps and bees suck the gravid rose.
Man dies, the hot sand cools,
Yesterday's sun is laid on a black stretcher.

The sweetness of nets, heavy honeycomb!
I am left with one aim,
A golden one: to free myself from the brunt of time.

I drink the turbid air as if it were dark water.
Time has been ploughed-up, the rose is earth.
The heavy-sweet roses whirled in a wreath!

[*from* 108]   1920

When Psyche, who is life, descends among the shades,
Following Persephone into half-transparent forest,
The blind swallow hurls itself at her feet
With Stygian affection and green twig.

Phantoms in a throng speed towards their new companion,
They meet the fugitive with lamentations,
In front of her they wring thin hands,
Perplexed with diffident expectations.

One holds out a mirror, another a phial of perfumes —
The soul likes trinkets, after all is feminine.
And dry complainings, like fine rain,
Sprinkle the leafless forest with transparent voices.

And not knowing what to do in this friendly hubbub,
The soul senses weight and size no longer.
She breathes on the mirror and is slow to hand over
The lozenge of copper to the master of the ferry.

[112]   1920

32

I have forgotten what I wanted to say.
The blind swallow flies back to her palace of shadows,
The empty boat sails up an arid estuary,
This night of frenzied absentmindedness.

Suddenly something grows, like tent or shrine,
Or a dead swallow falls to the earth,
A green twig twitching in its tender mouth.

O to bring back the bashfulness of seeing fingers,
Recognition's rounded happiness!
I am afraid of cracking like a bell.

They who are going to die can love and see,
Sound can be pouring through their fingers.
But I have forgotten what I wanted to say,
And a word without flesh flies back to its palace of shadows.

[*from* 113]   1920

Lightheartedly take from the palms of my hands
A little sun, a little honey,
As Persephone's bees commanded us.

Not to be untied, the unmoored boat;
Not to be heard, fur-shod shadows;
Not to be silenced, life's thick terrors.

Now we have only kisses,
Bristly and crisp like bees,
Which die as they fly from the hive.

They rustle in transparent thickets of night,
Their homeland thick forest of Taigetos,
Their food — honeysuckle, mint, and time.

Lightheartedly take then my uncouth present:
This simple necklace of dead, dried bees
Who once turned honey into sun.

[116]   1920

34

A golden sun, this is the Host,
Hung in air: where only Greek must sound,
This splendid moment:
The world an apple in your hand.

The solemn zenith of the service has begun,
Light in the circular temple, in July, under the dome,
So that wholeheartedly we sigh outside time
Over that meadowland where time does not run.

And the Eucharist hovers like an eternal midday —
All participate, play and sing.
In the eyes of all, the holy vessel is flowing
With never-ending gaiety.

[117]   1920

Because I had to let go your arms,
Because I turned traitor to your tender salty lips,
I must wait for dawn in the dense acropolis.
How I abhor these odorous ancient timbers.

Achaean men in the dark fit out the Horse,
Cut harshly into walls with toothed saws.
There is no way to lay the blood's dry murmur,
And for you no name, no sound, no sculpture.

How could I think that you would come back, how could
        I dare!
Why, before it was time, did I tear myself from you!
The black has not cleared, the cock has not crowed,
The hot axe not yet cut into wood.

The walls ooze resin like transparent tears,
The town feels its wooden ribs,
But blood has rushed to the attack, has gushed to the ladders,
And three times in dreams they kissed their own wives' lips.

Where is dear Troy? where the imperial, where the maidenly
        house?
Priam's lofty starling-coop will be a ruin.
And arrows fall like wooden un-wet rain,
And arrows, like a nut-grove, grow from the ground.

The last star-pricks are dying out painlessly
As morning, a grey swallow, raps at the window.
And lethargic day like an ox woken in straw
Stirs from long sleep across the rough haycocks.

[119]   1920

36

When the moon takes a walk along urban avenues,
And slowly lights the impenetrable town,
And darkness swells, full of melancholy and bronze,
And wax songs are smashed by the harshness of time;

And the cuckoo is weeping in its stone tower,
And the ashen one alights to reap lifeless worlds,
And quietly scattering huge spokes of shadow
Strews yellowing straw across the floorboards . . .

[121] 1920

Into the ring of dancing shadows
Which trampled down the tender meadow
I stepped with a song-like name.
Everything melted, there only remained
A mist of sound.
A few days, and I blended with the same,
Dissolved into favourite seraph or shadow.

And again wild fruit falls from the apple trees.

Happiness rolls by like a golden hoop
Fulfilling someone else's will,
And cutting the air with the palm of your hand
You chase the sweetness of Spring.

And it is so arranged that we do not dance away
From these spell-bound circles.
In virginal earth resilient hills
Lie swaddled away.

[*from* 123)   1920

from

POEMS

(1928)

I was washing — at night — in the courtyard,
The firmament harsh and bright;
Starlight like salt on an axe-blade;
The barrel, brim-full, is white.

A star melts — like salt — in the barrel;
The icy water is blacker;
Death more lucid, misfortune saltier, —
The earth more veracious, more awful.

[*from* 126]   1921

Winter — to some — is a blue sky of steaming wine & nuts,
A fragrant punch, to some, of cinnamon,
Some get their salty orders from the brutal stars
To carry back to smoke-filled huts.

A little still-warm chicken dung,
Sheep's muddle-headed warmth;
I will give everything for life, for cares
I need. A lighted match is enough for warmth.

Look: in my hand there is only an earthenware bowl;
A twittering prophecy of stars is tickling my thin ear;
Through this pitiful plumage I have to admire
The yellowness of grass & the warmth of the soil.

Quietly to be carding wool & tedding straw;
Like an apple-tree to starve in my winter binding;
Senselessly drawn by tenderness for every foreign thing;
Fumbling through emptiness, patiently waiting.

Let the conspirators hurry over the snow
Like sheep, let the brittle snow-crust crack;
Winter — to some — is a lodging of wormwood & acrid smoke,
To some the stern salt of solemn injury & lack.

O to raise a lantern on a long stick;
My dog in front, to walk under salt of stars
Into a soothsayer's yard, with a cock
For his cauldron. But the white, white snow makes my eyes smart.

[127]   1922

41

I climbed into the tousled hayloft,
Breathed the hay-dust of the mouldering stars,
The dishevelment of space,

And on the ladder pondered: why
Wake up a swarm of sounds, the miracle of Aeolian order,
Athwart this everlasting squabble?

Once again I would like to rustle-up something
Out of nothing,
To blaze like a match, give night a shove with my shoulder.

The huge and shaggy load sticks out above the universe,
The hayloft's ancient chaos
Begins to tickle as the darkness swells and rings.

Mowers bring back
Goldfinches fallen from their nests.
I will wring loose from these burning lines,

To the order of sound where I belong get back,
To the blood's grass-like and ringing connection,
Nerving myself for the dream beyond reason.

[*from* 131 and 132]   1922

MY TIME

My time, my brute, who could
Look you in the savage pupils of your eyes,
Glue together with his blood
The backbones of two centuries?
Blood the builder gushes
Out of the throat of earth's creatures;
But parasites tremble on the threshold of futures.

A creature, while alive,
Must bear his backbone:
Waves play on
His unseen spinal column.
Earth's infancy
Is the tender bones of a child,
A skull led to slaughter like a lamb.

To wrench our age out of prison
We need a flute to join
The joints of days now tumoured.
Waves of anguish rock
Our epoch,
In the grass an adder breathes
In time with golden measures.

And buds will swell again,
Shoots gush out greenly.
But your backbone is broken,
My beautiful, pitiful century.
With an idiot's harsh and feeble grin you look behind:
A beast who used to be cunning
Ponders the paw-marks in the sand.

[135]   1923

43

Poems published posthumously

ARMENIA

Clay, azure . . . azure, clay . . .
What more is needed? Squint quickly
Like a myopic shah over an enormous turquoise ring,
Over this book-like earth, a book that rings with clay,
A festering book, a costly clay
We are tormented by and stirred
As by music and the word.

[*part XIII of* 203–215]   1930

[THE AGE]

For the thunder & brilliance of eras to come,
For the glorious breed of lofty men,
I have relinquished the cup at the patriarchs-feast
And my happiness & my honour.

This world's wily wolf clutches my throat,
Though I am no wolf by blood;
Squeeze me instead like a hat up the sleeve
Of the hot fur-coat of the steppes:

Lest I see any tremble, & the slush & the mud,
And the blood-covered bones on the rack,
So (for me) all night blue polar foxes may shine
In their original beauty.

Show me the night by the shimmering river
Where pine-trees are worshipping stars:
I am no wolf by blood;
An equal only could break me.

[227]   1931

47

Preserve my words for ever for their aftertaste of misfortune
       & smoke,
Their pitch of careful labour, tar of perseverance.
So water in the wells of Novgorod should be sweet & black
To mirror a seven-spiked star at Christmas.

And for that — my begetter, partisan, harsh helper — ,
I (betrayer of the people's family, unacknowledged brother)
Promise to build the wells with timber thick enough
For princes to be lowered in buckets by the Tartars.

If these beheading-blocks befriended me: death in a garden,
       ninepins razed!
And for that, lifelong I will walk in an iron shirt
And find in the woods an axe —
To fondle for butchery, like Peter the Great.

[235]   1931

You took away my seas, & running jumps, & sky.
The violent earth tilted & opposed my feet.
Where could this stroke of genius get you?
You couldn't take away the mumble of my lips.

[307]   1935

Into the distance disappear the mounds of human heads.
I dwindle — go unnoticed now.
But in affectionate books, in children's games,
I will rise from the dead to say: the sun!

[341]   1937

49

Out of what ore
Could the dear yeast of the earth restore
Sounds, tears and toil,
The drizzle of stress,
Troubles on the boil,
Or all lost accents?

For the first time in your beggar's mind
You sniff out raw craters,
Copper-coloured waters:
On foot,
Self-hating, self-ignorant,
The blind leading the blind.

[347]   1937

I look into the frost's face, alone:
It's going nowhere,
Which is where I come from.
Miraculous! The breathing plain all ironed,
Without a crease.
The sun screws up its eyes in laundered destitution,
Finds calm and consolation . . .
Innocent as bread, snow crunches in my eyes.

[*from* 349]   1937

Asthmatic sloth of the steppes!
Sickened by space — I am choking!
The pulsating horizon swells up; a bandage could help me —
By blinding.

I would prefer to have borne the disposition in leaf-like layers
Of sand on toothy shores.
I would have clung to the shy sleeves of rivers,
Their ripples, brinks & holes.

We would have worked in harmony — a hundred years,
        a moment's flash in the dark.
Envious of the precipitation of the rapids,
I would have listened under drifting bark
To the fibrous procession of the rings.

[351]   1937

[LIFE IS MATCHLESS]

With tender terror as my bodyguard
I yield to the plainness of these plains,
Which level everything.
The sky's sphere sickens me, is my undoing.

I appealed to the air, my servant,
Waiting for service or news;
I gathered for a journey, swam into arcs
Of voyages which would never start.

I am ready to wander where I will have more sky.
But that bright longing cannot release me now
From Voronezh's still-young hills
To the bright, all-human ones of Tuscany.

[352]   1937

What has contended with oxide and alloys
Burns like feminine silver,
And quiet work silvers
The iron plough and voice of the poem-maker.

[353]   1937

I still have not died. Still not alone,
With a beggar-woman for companion,
I am delighted by the immense plains,
And the haze, and hunger, and snow-storms.

In dreadful joy, lovely poverty,
I live — alone and peaceful and consoled:
These days and nights are blessed,
This sinless labour honey-voiced.

Unhappy he whom, like his shadow,
The dog's bark scares and the wind makes hay of.
And poor indeed he who half-alive
Begs favour of a shadow.

[354]   1937

As a pebble from the sky hurtling downwards
Bangs the earth awake somewhere or other,
The verse fell, disgraced, father unknown:
Inexorable, the meteors of the maker.
You cannot judge windfalls — they can be no other.

[357]   1937

I hear, I hear the early ice
Rustle under bridges,
And remember bright-coloured drunkenness
Drift over us.

From stale stairways, from areas
Of awkward palaces
Circling his Florence
Alighieri sang with more power
From tired lips.

So too my shadow picks
With eyes at grain of granite,
Sees in the dark a row of logs:
Seeming houses in the light.

Or twiddles its thumbs, is lazy,
Yawns,
Is noisy,
Basking in other people's wine and sky,

And feeds stale loaves
To the importunate swans . . .

[358] 1937

LINES CONCERNING
THE UNKNOWN SOLDIER

(1)

Let this air be a witness —
His long-range omniverous heart —
All-poisoning even in the action of the
        dug-out —
Is water, is windowless substance

The stars are the informers of the sky:
They need to see everything — why? —
To condemn the judge and the witness,
Into the water, the windowless substance

Rain, a sullen sower,
And his nameless manna;
A wood of crosses to remember
Ocean and battle-field

Men will freeze and hunger,
Will kill, sicken and starve,
And in his well-known grave
Unknown will be laid the soldier

Teach me, unwell swallow, now you've
        unlearnt to fly:
No wing, no rudder,
To master
This ground-less airy grave

(2)

These worlds threaten us
Like rustling grapes,
They hang like stolen cities,
Like golden stars, slurs,
Slips of the tongue, slanders

(8)

Arteries juicy with blood.
A murmur resounds through the ranks:
— I was born in '94,
I was born in '92 . . .
And, clutching the worn-out year of my birth,
I whisper through anaemic lips:
I was born in the night of January the 2nd and 3rd
In the unreliable year
Of eighteen ninety something or other, and
The centuries surround me with fire

[*from parts* 1, 2 and 8 of 362]   1937

[MY HEIRS]

Tongue-tied, dumb & language-less:
All singularity is gone.
No longer me singing, — but whatever breathes — ,
My ears sheathed in mountains, numb, & hearing-less.

A single-eyed song grown out of moss & air,
A single-voiced offering
Chanted on horses, on hills:
Hunters make good their title to take in air.

A vexed & generous justice is their care:
To betroth & bring
The young pair — sinless —
To their wedding . . .

[*from* 365]   1937

Breaks of the rounded bays, of shingle & cartilage & blue,
And the slow sail continued by a cloud —
I am parted from you, scarcely having known your worth:
Longer than organ fugues & bitter is the sea-grass,
Which looks like hair but isn't & smells of long-contracted lies.
My head is tipsy with an iron tenderness,
Rust gnaws gently at the sloping shore . . .
Why does another sand lie under my head?
You — guttural Urals, muscular Volga land,
These steppes — here are all my rights, —
And I must go on breathing you, full-lunged.

[366]   1937

Armed with the eyesight and absorption of wasps
Which suck and sip earth's axis, axis,
I swallow everything I have to witness,
Grasp it, fruitlessly, by heart.

I don't paint, don't sing,
Don't rasp a black-voiced bow across a string:
I only sting the living,
And envy the energy of subtle wasps.

Oh if only some day — avoiding sleep and death —
A ray of air, the pierce of summer's fervour,
Could make me hear the
Buzz of earth, buzz of the earth . . .

[367]   1937

Eyes keener than sharpened scythes —
In the pupil a cuckoo and a drop of dew, —

Barely able — stretched to full stature —
To see the solitary multitude of stars.

[368]   1937

I'm in a lion's trench, plunged in a fort,
And sinking lower, lower, lower,
Under the yeast shower of these sounds:
More trenchant than lions, more potent than the Pentateuch.

How close your summons:
Keener than commandments of childbirth, firstlings — ,
Like strings of pearls at the bottom of the sea
Or meek baskets borne by Gauguin's mistresses.

Motherland of chastening songs, approach,
With the declivities deepening in your voice! — O primal mother,
The shy-sweet icon-faces of *our* daughters
Are not worth your little finger.

My time is still unbounded.
And I have accompanied the rapture of the universe
As muted organ pipes
Accompany a woman's voice.

[370]   1937

If our antagonists take me
And people stop talking with me;
If they confiscate the whole world —
The right to breathe & open doors
And affirm that existence will exist
And that the people, like a judge, will judge;
If they dare to keep me like an animal
And fling my food on the floor —
I won't fall silent or deaden the agony,
But will write what I am free to write,
And yoking ten oxen to my voice
Will move my hand in the darkness like a plough
And fall with the full heaviness of the harvest . . .

[*from* 372]   1937

[CATHEDRAL]

I saw a lake, standing sheer,
A cut rose in a circuit,
Fishes finning through their fresh water arbour.

Plagues glared through three barking portals,
A gazelle leapt down a violet span,
The cliff sighed suddenly with towers.

And slaked with liquid the candid sandstone rose,
An ocean-urchin swollen sweetly from a river
To hurl up chalices of water to the clouds.

[*from* 374]   1937

[UNDONE]

So in cathedrals
Of extraordinarily-vivid crystals, sun-spiders unbind all ribs
To spin their bundles:
Life is scrupulously ravelled.

An exact shaft of sun to join them,
The bonds of neat lines being thankful enough
Will gather, intimate, somewhere or other,
Like guests with the masks off.

Only now, on earth, and not in heaven,
As in a house suffused with music. —
If only we don't scare or wound or sicken them.
— Fine if we could live till then.

Forgive me for telling you this.
Quietly read it through to me.

[*from* 380]   1937

WINEJUG

Venal procurer of water & wine,
Envenomed flutes whine, bode bad & gloat
(Goats prancing, fruits falling, to the music of the vine)
Because of the ruin that looms on your black-red rim:
And no one to undertake it,
No one to lay the harm.

[*from* 383]   1937

O how much I would like —
Seen by nobody —
To soar behind the light,
To disappear utterly.

But you, encircle yourself with light —
There is no other rapture, no other trance.
And learn from the stars
What light is all about.

You, whom I want to delight —
This is a whisper:
In a lullaby,
Little one, I hand you to the light.

It must be an arrow of light,
When murmurs —
The babble of sweethearts —
Ardently set it alight.

[384]   1937

This azure island was exalted by its potters —
Crete the gay. In the resounding earth
They baked their gift. Do you hear the dolphin fins
Thrust under earth?

Speak of the sea
In the kiln baked happy,
The cold power of the pot
Clove into sea, into eye.

Azure island, give me back what is mine —
My labour — , from the breasts
Of the fruitful goddess
Fill the white-hot pots.

This was, turned azure, & was chanted,
Long before Ulysses,
Before drink, before food,
Were called 'my' or 'mine' across these seas.

Convalesce & shine again,
Luminary of ox-eyed heaven,
And fortuity, the flying fish,
And the water saying 'yes'.

[385]   1937

Thalassa & thanatos of Grecian flutes:
The babble of remembering lips that pined —
Uncodified, unconscious — ,
Crossed ditches, which ripened.

The flute player never knows repose —
It seems he is alone,
That sometime or other out of lilac clay
He moulded seas which are his own.

Later he will not be repeated,
Clods of clay to knead in the hands of the sea.
And I, when I am filled with the sea,
My measure is mortality.

My own lips lisp,
Disease or a killing at the root.
And involuntarily falling, falling,
I diminish the force of the flute.

[*from* 387]   1937

I raise this greenness to my lips,
This sticky promise of leaves,
This breach-of-promise earth:
Mother of maples, of oaks, of snowdrops.

See how I'm dazzled, exalted,
Obedient to the lowliest root;
And are not my eyes miraculously
Blinded by this bright tree!

The croaking of green frogs concatenates
Like balls of mercury;
Twigs are growing into branches;
The fallow air is milky.

[388]   1937

The pear tree,
The bird-cherry tree
            Took aim at me
Their subtle strength
            Hit the target
                    Me

            Leaves radiate like
Stars, blossom
            In clusters
What is this two-fold power?
            Which are truth's
                    Flowers?

            The air's
Murderous eye
            Wages
War
            With white
                    Power

            Charm
Of this fragrance
            (Blending impossibly)
Reaches out, struggling,
            Blurring
                    Abruptly

[*from* 393]   1937

With her irregular delightful way of walking
She is limping on the empty earth;
A constrained freedom
Of animating deficiency
Draws her on. And it seems that a clear surmise
Lingers in her way of walking —
Something to do with this Spring weather,
Original mother of the sepulchral dome.
And this will eternally be beginning.

There are women who are natives of the sodden earth:
Their every step a hollow sobbing,
Their calling to accompany the dead,
To be first to meet the risen.
And we would trespass to demand caresses of them,
And to part from them is beyond our strength.
Today — angel, tomorrow — the sepulchral worm,
The day after — a stark outline, —
What was a step, now beyond us . . .

But waiting for us
Is only a promise.

[*from* 394]   1937

Appendix

NOTE: I have relegated to an appendix this poem which Clarence Brown has called 'one of [Mandelstam's] greatest masterpieces': I should be cheating if I tried to pass my version off as an adequate rendering. The original (unrhymed) poem is held together by echolalia — the repetition of similar sounds (sh-r-kh) which cannot be re-enacted in English, at least by me. But — for what it's worth — here is my attempt.

THE MAN WHO FOUND A HORSESHOE

We look at the forest and say:
Here is a forest of ships and masts,
Red pines
To creak in the storm,
In the furious forestless air;
The plumbline, fastened to the dancing deck, will hold out
        under the wind's salt heel.
And the sea-wanderer,
In his unbridled thirst for space,
Dragging through damp ruts a geometer's fragile equipment,
Collates the rough surface of the seas
With the attraction of the earth's lap.

But breathing the smell
Of resinous tears oozing through planks,
Admiring the riveted boards
Of bulkheads,
We say:
These too stood on the earth,
Awkward as a donkey's backbone,
Their crests forgetful of their roots,

69

On a famous mountain ridge,
And howled under the sweet cloud-burst,
Fruitlessly offering the sky their precious freight
For a pinch of salt.

Where shall we begin?
Everything pitches and cracks,
The air quivering with comparisons,
The earth buzzing with metaphors.
And light two-wheeled chariots,
Harnessed brightly to a flock of strenuous birds,
Explode,
Vying with the snorting favourites of the race-track.

Three-times blessed who puts a name into song;
A song adorned with a name
Is marked by a head-band
Which stops it swooning from stupefying smells,
Whether the nearness of man,
Fur of beast,
Or simply a whiff of thyme rubbed in the palms.

The air dark like water, everything alive swims in it like fish
Undulating through the sphere,
Compact, resilient, hardly-heated —
A crystal in which wheels move, horses shy,
The humid black-earth every night thrown up anew
By pitchforks, hoes and ploughs.
The air is mixed as densely as the earth, —
You can't get out, to enter it is arduous.

Rustling runs through the trees like a green ball-game;
Children playing knucklebones with the vertebrae of dead
        animals.
The fragile reckoning of our era comes to an end.
Let us be grateful for what we had:

I too made mistakes, lost my way, embroiled myself in the
      accounts.
The era rang like a golden globe,
Cast, hollow, supported by no one.
Touched, it answered 'yes' and 'no',
As a child will say:
'I'll give you an apple', or: 'I won't give you one.'
Its face an exact copy of the voice which pronounces these
      words.

The sound is still ringing although its cause has stopped.
The horse foams in the dust.
But the acute curve of his neck
Preserves the memory of the race with blazing legs
When there were as many horses as stones on the road.

And so,
The one who has found a horseshoe
Blows away the dust,
Rubs it with wool till it shines,
Then
Hangs it over the threshold
To rest,
No longer to strike sparks.
Human lips
            which have nothing more to say
Keep the shape of the last word said.
And the arm retains the sense of weight
Though the jug
          splashed half-empty
                    on the way home.

What I am saying at this moment is not being said by me
But is dug from the ground like grains of petrified wheat.

Some
      on their coins depict lions,
Others
      a head;
Various tablets of gold, brass and bronze
Lie with equal honour in the earth.
The century, trying to bite through them, left its
      teeth-marks there.
Time clips me like a coin,
And there's no longer enough of me left for myself.

[*from* 136]   1923

Notes

In this rag-bag of notes I have set out to refer to and convey as wide a spectrum of information as is succinctly possible; I have purposely excluded commentaries of my own, because the act of translation is necessarily an act of literary criticism, and my judgements, my knowledge and ignorance, are embodied in my renderings.

Numbers refer to those underneath each poem.

J.G.

STONE (1913)

Stone, the title of Mandelstam's first book of poems, 'is obviously a prosaic symbol, yet timeless and in a way sacred — the material of which streets and cathedrals are made' (N. A. Nilsson, *Scando-Slavica* IX).

(14) Fyodor Tyutchev (1803–1873) also wrote a celebrated poem called *Silentium*. In Charles Tomlinson's version (*Versions from Fyodor Tyutchev* by Charles Tomlinson, Oxford University Press, 1960) it runs as follows:

> Be silent, hide yourself:
> In the still spirit
> Hoard those hauntings
> And let their coming
> Be like the speechlessness of stars
> By night-time waking, rising, homing.
>
> What temerity may sound
> Another's depth, survey its ground?
> Utter your thoughts
> They flow in lies. Dig down
> You cloud the spring that feeds the silences.
>
> Learn to live in yourself. There
> Thought on thought,
> Fretful of glare and stir,
> Begets its untold transmutations
> And their song
> Only in silence may you hear.

(31) The poet Batyushkov (1787–1855) spent the last thirty or so years of his life in an asylum (from 1821).

73

(39) A poem, for Mandelstam, 'is a structure of words that support and oppose each other, as a cathedral is a structure of stones that support each other' (Clarence Brown, *Mandelstam*, Cambridge University Press, 1973, p. 148).

(54) Joseph: Osip is a Russian version of Joseph.

TRISTIA (1922)

Tristia, the title of Mandelstam's second book of poems, 'is a lament and encomium for a splendid past, for Renaissance Venice, for Racine's France, for Hellas, above all for Petropolis, the classical Petersburg of Derzhavin and Pushkin. These cultures are seen as one, are fused into one . . . image of threatened civilisation . . . The theme of *Tristia* is summed up in a line of Mandelstam's poem about Venice: "How can I escape this festive death?" ' (Robert Chandler, from an unpublished article on Mandelstam and Ezra Pound).

(82) Troezen was where Hippolytus died. Clarence Brown (*Mandelstam*): 'I know nothing, by the way, of the missing lines 7 and 8.'

(84) This poem refers to one of the Kremlin churches (the Cathedral of the Assumption) built by Italian architects in the 15th century. I am indebted to Henry Gifford for the information that, in the last stanza, 'Aurora' refers to Marina Tsvetaeva, who wore a fur-coat at this time when showing Mandelstam round Moscow.

(89) 'Petropolis': St Petersburg or Petrograd.

(90) A poem dedicated to Marina Tsvetaeva.

(92) Tauris: the Crimea.

(93) '[Mandelstam's] visions of classical antiquity are not "Homeric", "Sapphic", or "Horatian", but Mandelstamian . . . It is "world culture", not ancient culture, that is the leitmotif of M's poetry' (Victor Terras, 'Classical motifs in the poetry of Osip Mandelstam', *Slavic and East European Journal*, 3 (1966), 251–67).

Persephone (or Kore or Proserpina), Queen of the Underworld, spends two-thirds of the year with her mother Demeter (the Greek corn-goddess). 'This is the "light" part of the annual circle . . .' The black sail is 'still another topos of Greek mythology, known best from the myth of Theseus and Ariadne' (Victor Terras).

74

Line 20: 'Black rose-flakes' is a reference to Mandelstam's mother's death (see N. Mandelstam, *Hope Abandoned*, Collins and Harvill, 1974).

(104) Compare: 'In the stillness of night a lover pronounces one tender name instead of another, and suddenly realises that this has happened once before: the words and the hair and the cock who has just crowed under the window crowed already in Ovid's *Tristia*. And he is overcome by a deep joy of recognition . . .' (Osip Mandelstam, 'The Word and Culture', in *Sobraniye sochineniy*, Inter-Language Literary Associates, Washington, Vol. 2, revised ed., 1967).

Stanza 3: Clarence Brown refers to 'the special kind of cognition that takes place when a poet composes a poem. Mandelstam declares that this is in fact *recognition*' ('*Mandelstam's Notes Towards a Supreme Fiction*', *Delos*, Austin, Texas, 1968, No. I).

Line 25 onwards: see Pushkin, *Yevgeny Onegin* V:4–10. 'The method [of divination] was to melt a candle into a shallow dish of water, where the suddenly cooled wax would assume odd shapes like Rorschach blots or . . . like a cloud or the stretched pelt of a squirrel . . . Ovid's parting from his loved ones as he goes into exile is a paradigm of all partings' (Clarence Brown, *Mandelstam*, p. 274).

Erebus: name of 'a place of darkness between Earth and Hades'. Erebus is the son of Chaos, brother of Night, and father of Day.

(108) Line 3 refers to the death of Pushkin.

(116) Bees were sacred to Persephone. 'The poet as a bee that makes honey is a recurrent image in Mandelstam' (Sidney Monas, see below).

Taigetos: the high mountain overlooking Sparta, the domain of Artemis.

(119) Line 16: Sea the *Odyssey*, Book IV:
Right well, (replied the king) your speech displays
The matchless merit of the chief you praise:
Heroes in various climes myself have found,
For martial deeds, and depth of thought renown'd.
But Ithacus, unrival'd in his claim,
May boast a title to the loudest fame:
In battle calm, he guides the rapid storm,
Wise to resolve, and patient to perform.
What a wondrous conduct in the chief appear'd,
When the vast fabric of the steed we rear'd!
Some demon, anxious for the Trojan doom,

Urged you with great Deiphobus to come,
To explore the fraud; with guile opposed to guile,
Slow-pacing thrice around the insidious pile,
Each noted leader's name you thrice invoke,
Your accent varying as their spouses spoke:
The pleasing sounds each latent warrior warm'd,
But most Tydides' and my heart alarmed:
To quit the steed we both impatient press,
Threatening to answer from the dark recess.
Unmoved the mind of Ithacus remain'd,
And the vain ardours of our love restrain'd:
But Anticlus, unable to control,
Spoke loud the language of his yearning soul:
Ulysses straight with indignation fired,
(For so the common care of Greece required)
Firm to his lips his forceful hands applied,
Till on his tongue the fluttering murmurs died.
Meantime Minerva from the fraudful horse
Back to the court of Priam bent your course.

(Alexander Pope)

POEMS (1928)

'Mandelstam's *Poems* 1921–25 register a disintegration so absolute
that the magnificent tragedy of *Tristia* is no longer possible, for
tragedy presupposes the existence of generally accepted values'
(Robert Chandler).

(127) Stanza 5 — 'conspirators': the Soviet edition substitutes the word
used in Russian for 'people'.

(136) See Appendix. '. . . this is an ode (Mandelstam first subtitled
it "a Pindaric fragment"), and, typically of the ode, it is con-
cerned with itself, that is to say, with poetry. The world in which
poetry must now exist is as turbulent as that of the forest and
ship: Everything cracks and shakes . . . The principal image of
the poem, the horseshoe itself, is what is *left* of the stormy animal,
now dead . . . This is human life frozen in its last attitudes, as
though surprised in Herculaneum. The speaker himself now
speaks in a resurrected voice, turned to stone, and time, the ele-
ment that erupted . . . at line 55, finally flows like lava over
everything, obliterating the very self of the speaker at the end.'
(Clarence Brown, *Mandelstam.*)

76

(235) 'Novgorod': 'The medieval Russian merchant-republic, con-
quered and repressed by Ivan III in 1478, with terrible destruc-
tion, losing its former autonomy. It was destroyed again by Ivan
IV (the Terrible) for dealing with the state of Poland-Lithuania,
and severely repressed once more in 1650 for protests against the
coinage. Novgorod, which in its heyday as an independent re-
public had been a member of the Hanseatic League, came to
represent the Western orientation in Russia, and its aspirations
to democracy. This was the significance it had for the nineteenth-
century Decembrists and later liberals. It was also the home of
religious heresy, and the scene of repression of religious dissent
by Muscovy. All these connotations are present here, as well as
the prophecies proclaiming the resurrection of Novgorod. The
poem has other associations with political tyranny, repression,
and the suffering of oppression: punishment inflicted by the
Tartars during the period of the Mongol Yoke on those Russian
princes who failed to obey their edicts or meet their tax quotas
or resisted them in any way.

'The iron shirt — a quaint form of medieval torture; also a form
of askesis practised by the *iurodivye*, or "Fools in Christ."

'Peter the Great was a do-it-yourselfer and learned how to shave
beards, pull teeth, and also to chop off heads; he performed several
of his own executions. In the face of oppression, Mandelstam as-
sumes the role of the *iurodivy*, the Holy Fool, imitator of Christ.'
(Sidney Monas, from Notes to *Complete Poetry of Mandelstam*,
translated by Burton Raffel and Alla Burago, State University of
New York Press, Albany 1973.)

The rest of the poems printed here were all composed in exile in
Voronezh. 'During the years in Voronezh Mandelstam, like Pound
in the Detention Camp at Pisa, knowing that he might die at any
moment . . . looked at the world for the last, as though for the
first, time' (Robert Chandler). Of the Voronezh poems Donald
Rayfield has said: 'The poet as a thinker, as an incarnation of the
Hellenic spirit, barely functions. He is only an eye bewildered by
forests, rivers, earth, wooden houses, the open spaces and the
boundless sky of the steppes, which itself seems to him to be an
eye on a cosmic plane. His thoughts are paralysed by an instinctive
feeling of a predator's presence, the Kremlin which is now the
axis on which the poet's world rotates' ('Mandelstam's Voronezh
poetry', *Russian Literature Triquarterly*, 1975); 'the poetry of
1933 and afterwards has a posthumous quality, breathing borrowed air on borrowed time' (*Grosseteste Review*, Vol. 7, Nos
1–3, 'Deaths and Resurrections: The Later Poetry of Osip Mandelstam').

(307) 'Feet': 'the human and the metric foot which must both walk the black earth' (Donald Rayfield).

(347) The 'dear yeast of the earth' is of course poetry.

(354) 3rd stanza, line 4: the 'shadow' Mandelstam might have 'begged favour of' alludes to Stalin.

(358) Henry Gifford (in a letter to me); 'The "stale loaves" suggest to me Dante's bread that tastes of salt, or what is called in *Richard II* "the bitter bread of banishment".'

(362) Here 'he speaks not of his own death, but of the coming of an entire era of wholesale annihilation, in which everyone dies "herded with the herd" . . . and becomes an "unknown soldier", the author himself among them' (N. Mandelstam, *Hope Abandoned*, Collins and Harvill, 1974). Donald Rayfield has pointed out to me the (untranslatable) puns and anagrams in line 4 of the first stanza: *okean* (ocean), *okno* (window), and *yest'* (to eat/ and there is/there are), *veshchestvo* (substance).

(366) 'Urals': In 1934 Mandelstam was exiled to the Urals, to Cherdyn (where – thinking he was going to be arrested again – he threw himself out of the window of the hospital he was in), and travelled along the Volga to arrive there.

'These steppes' refers to Voronezh.

I am indebted to Robert Chandler for drawing my attention to the fact that 'Here are all my rights' refers to Pushkin's poem *From Piedmont* (1836), in which Pushkin says he doesn't mind about censorship, not having the right to vote, etc.; all he cares about is that he should be left to himself, not have to give account to others of what he does, and be free to wonder at the godlike beauties of nature and art: 'Here is my happiness! Here are my rights . . .'

(367) This poem was written during the time when Mandelstam was particularly obsessed with Joseph Stalin. Wasp, in Russian, is *osa*, axis is *os*. Joseph, in Russian, can be either O*sip* or I*osif*.

(368) The last poem in Mandelstam's Stalin cycle. The cuckoo, as also in "the cuckoo is weeping in its stone tower' (No. 121), alludes to a passage from *The Lay of Igor's Campaign*, a 12th century poem in which Yaroslavna, Igor's wife, mourns him 'like a desolate cuckoo'. 'On the Danube Yaroslavna's voice is heard; like a desolate cuckoo she cries early in the morning. "I will fly," she says, "like a cuckoo along the Danube, I will dip my sleeve of beaver-fur in the river Kayala, I will wipe the Prince's bleeding wounds . . ." ' (*Penguin Book of Russian Verse*, ed. Obolensky,

p. 18). '[M] lamented his failing eyesight, which had once been "sharper than a whetted scythe" but had not had time to pick out each of the "lonely multitude of stars".' (Nadezhda Mandelstam, *Hope Against Hope*, Collins and Harvill, 1972, p. 202).

(370) 'Speaking of himself, he used here the "inexorable past tense" . . . A few more months were to pass, and he would say to Akhmatova: "I am ready for death".' (Nadezhda Mandelstam, *Hope Against Hope*, p. 202).

(373) '. . . the last appearance of Notre Dame in M's poetry . . . the poem is not, like "Notre Dame" [No. 39], a notation of immediate vision. It is rather like the assembled shards of some fragmented dream, important pieces of which are missing" (Clarence Brown, *Mandelstam*, p. 192). Clarence Brown informs me that in fact Mandelstam had in mind two other Gothic cathedrals (Rheims and Laon) as well.

(384) 'Pound's and Mandelstam's verse is a medium of perception and exploration, and, even when they write of chaos and emptiness, is a source of light' (Robert Chandler).

(385) Line 8: 'Presumably this means that the pot split into the two aspects of poetry: the raw material — the sea which gave birth to Aphrodite — and the forming, shaping poetic eye' (Donald Rayfield, private communication).

(387) Thalassa: sea; thanatos: death. 'The Greek flute's sounds are clearly the poetic force before it has been precipitated in language . . . [The] flute's music . . . crosses barriers, it is unselfconscious . . . The poet creates his own past; "making his native sea" out of clay, like the Cretan potters . . . [But] the flautist is in the past, unrepeatable. He is what the poet might have been or continued being, had the Hellenic world not fallen apart. Now nothing works: the sea gives no birth . . . [it] kills instead of giving life . . . [Mandelstam's] lips cannot work the flute, and the balance of forces . . . topples, leaving only the destructive, negative force to silence poetry . . . If there is a moral in the poem, it is that the poet conscious of his individual death is tainted by his fear and loses his gift of immersing himself in the medium of poetry.' (Donald Rayfield, *Russian Literature Triquarterly*.)

(393) In a playful poem written two days earlier to celebrate the forthcoming marriage of Natasha Shtempel there is a line about pear trees. As Donald Rayfield has said (see above) Mandelstam 'starts personifying nature, and then identifying it with Natasha Shtempel and her life.'

(394) The limping woman was also Natasha Shtempel, whom the Mandelstams knew in Voronezh.

Credits: Passages from published work by the following are reprinted in the Notes above by permission: Charles Tomlinson, *Versions from Fyodor Tyutchev* (Oxford University Press, London and New York); Clarence Brown, *Mandelstam* (Cambridge University Press, London and New York); Victor Terras, 'Classical motifs in the poetry of Osip Mandelstam' (*Slavic and East European Journal*); Sidney Monas, Notes to *Complete Poetry of Osip Mandelstam*, translated by Burton Raffel and Alla Burago (by permission of the State University of New York Press; Copyright 1973 State University of New York); Nadezhda Mandelstam, *Hope Against Hope* and *Hope Abandoned* (Copyright 1970 and 1972 by Atheneum Publishers; English translation Copyright 1970 and 1973, 1974 by Atheneum Publishers, New York and Harvill Press Ltd, London, respectively; published by Atheneum Publishers, New York and William Collins Sons & Co. Ltd, London); Dimitri Obolensky, *The Penguin Book of Russian Verse* (Penguin Books Ltd; Copyright Dimitri Obolensky, 1962, 1963). See also the acknowledgements made on pages 17–18 of this book.

THIS BOOK was typeset in linotype and foundry Janson — a type originally cut in Amsterdam in 1690 by Nicholas Kis, a Hungarian. The name of the typeface is therefore misleading, as it was not cut by Anton Janson, the well known Dutch type designer of this period who worked in Leipzig.

Composed by American Book–Stratford Press, Inc., Brattleboro, Vermont.

Printed by Thomson–Shore, Inc., Dexter, Michigan.

Designed by Julia Runk and Hazel Bercholz.